AN INTRODUCTION TO PRACTICAL

PAINT**EFFECTS**

IDEAS AND TECHNIQUES TO TRANSFORM YOUR HOME

STEPHANIE BAKER

AN INTRODUCTION TO PRACTICAL

PAINTER

IDEAS

AND

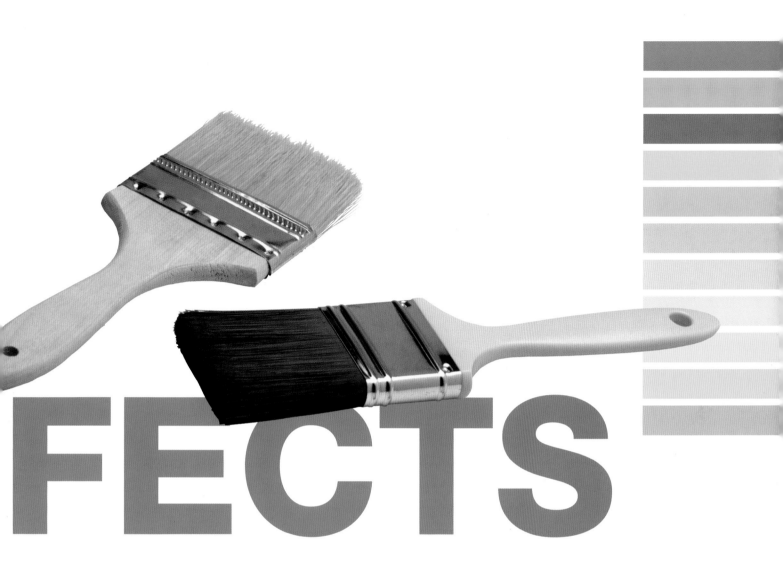

FECTS

TECHNIQUES TO TRANSFORM YOUR HOME

LIFESTYLE

Contents

Publisher: Lisa Simpson

Designer: Emily Cook

Picture researcher: Sarah Epton

This edition first published in Great Britain in 2000 by

LifeStyle

An imprint of Parkgate Books

London House, Great Eastern Wharf, Parkgate Road,

London SW11 4NQ

Projects featured in this book have previously appeared in

Simply Paint by Linda Barker and Simply Stencilling by Linda Barker

Published by Anaya

© Parkgate Books

A Division of Collins and Brown

A CIP catalogue record for this book is available from

the British Library.

ISBN 1-902617-16-9

PRINTED AND BOUND IN CHINA

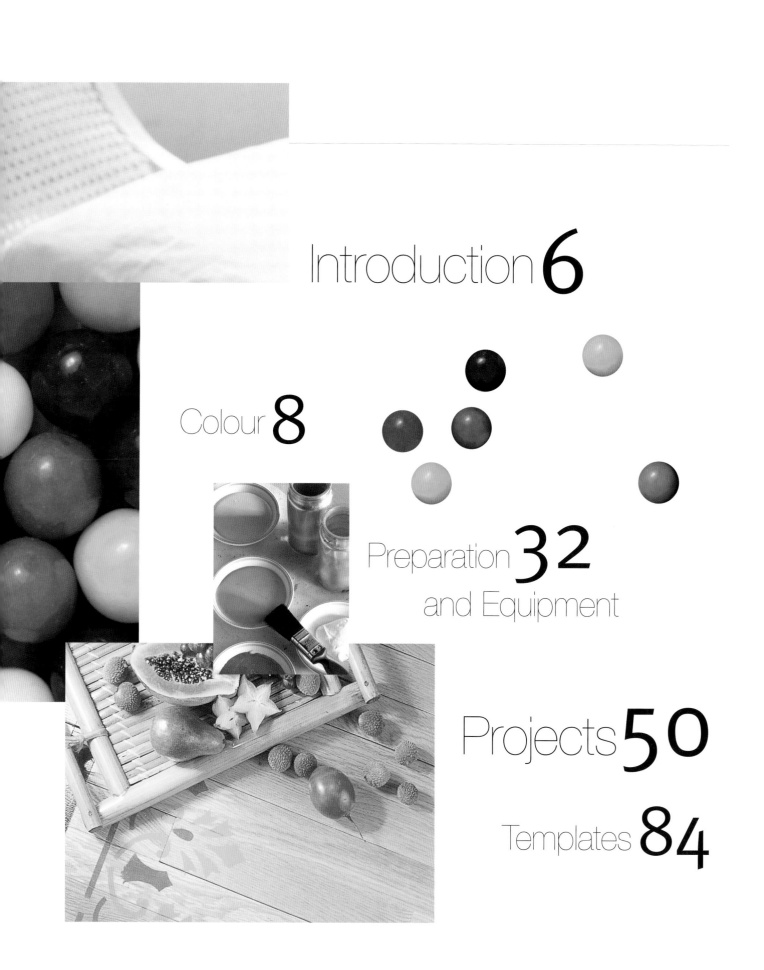

Introduction 6

Colour 8

Preparation 32
and Equipment

Projects 50

Templates 84

Introduction

When you enter a **room** for the first time it's decor, whether pastel or vivid, will capture your attention immediately. Colour washed or sponged walls, stencilled borders or wood grained furniture are the decorative details that can transform a house into a **home** by adding style and character.

The appearance of your home will carry your own personality and the simple addition of **colour** and texture will enable you to truly express yourself. Different rooms in your house will have different priorities and purposes, so you will need to take into account the overall mood you wish to convey.

We often have an **idea** in our minds of how we would like our home or pieces of furniture to look but think that the work involved in transforming this into a reality is a skill that we don't possess.

All too often, paint effects are seen as too complicated or **artistic** for many to implement but this book will introduce you to a wide variety of methods in detail, providing step-by-step instructions on how to achieve the perfect **result**. Paint offers limitless possibilities and the techniques selected in this book offer an opportunity for you to **transform** your home.

Stephanie Baker

Colour

One of the main ingredients in decorating successfully

is to make the best use of colour. The right colour can

add interest to a drab room, light to a dark room or a

sense of calm to a busy room. Colour can make a cold

room appear warmer, a small room appear larger and a

large room cosier.

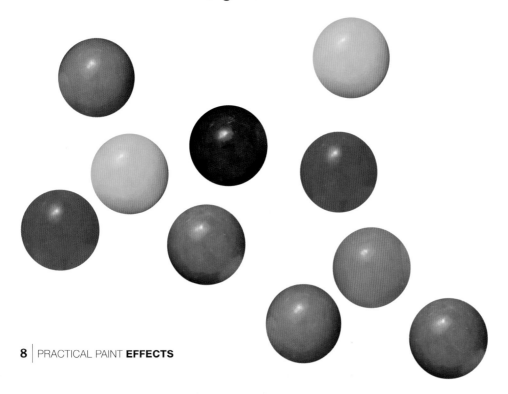

Colour

Learning the basics about colour is the first step to understanding colour and how best to use it. Given that the human eye can recognise around 7 million colours, it is little wonder that confusion can set in. This results in many of us taking the safe option as we are afraid of making mistakes and the expense involved in having to rectify these mistakes.

Another factor that needs to be taken into consideration is the effect of light – either natural or artificial – on colour. For instance, a South facing room will receive more natural daylight so colours will appear more vibrant, whereas a North facing room with a colder light makes colours appear less intense.

The colours that you choose for your home do not only reflect your personal taste but they are also tools for influencing the mood and atmosphere of a room. Colours are susceptible to trends, as much as say clothes and music, and you should take this into account unless you want to redecorate every season.

There are thousands of colours to choose from, so a good starting point would be to choose the style of room you would like and then to look for colours that are associated with or compliment that particular theme.

Colour can evoke many different moods and the paint you select will help to create your chosen ambience. Other important factors to take into account are lighting, furniture and soft furnishings and there may be particular features that you wish to emphasize and others you wish to hide.

Colour

Colours can be used to create mood and to alter our perceptions of space. Consider what the room will be used for when deciding on the colour scheme. You can combine colours to create the required effect following the principles of complementary and related colours, warm and cool colours and light and dark colours.

As a rule, warm colours evoke a cosy, intimate mood and cool colours, a tranquil mood. However, you can combine colours to create other effects. For example, red details in a blue room will make the cool, tranquil room feel warmer and both colours will appear more vibrant. The lightness and darkness of colours can affect mood, too. Deep yellow will produce a more intimate effect than pale lemon.

One of the most amazing aspects of colour is the way it can visually change the shape and size of a room. If a room is painted with a light colour, the walls will seem to recede, creating the impression of a larger space. Cool colours will achieve the same effect. You can create the opposite effect by using dark or warm colours.

When selecting paint colours, it is very important to consider the dominant colours in the existing furnishings, or in those, which you plan to add to the room. Just as the colours of the walls and the woodwork should harmonize, so should the painted surfaces, the furniture, pictures, curtains and floor coverings. Often, new furniture or carpeting calls for repainting the room.

Consider any other objects in the room, which will have to harmonize with the paint colours you have chosen, for instance, natural-wood furniture and a wooden floor will create a feeling of warmth in a room.

All colours are derived from just three primary colours – red, blue and yellow – which are blended and mixed to create a multitude of different combinations.

Red

Sultry and **scintillating** red defines and fills any space, large or small and can have the effect of making a room seem smaller and more **intimate**. It heightens the senses, conjuring images of hot chillies, bullfights and bravery. Definitely not for the timid, red brings a sense of the **dramatic** to any room, although its variants can create wildly different moods – for instance the innocence of pink and the mysteries of a deep purple.

Blue

Cool blue carries with it the harmonies and **balance** of the sea and sky and mixes these characteristics with a deliberateness that pulls the eye into it, but leaves the impression of **space** and **openness**. Blue provides comfort and assurance, conveying an overall sense of calm and **tranquillity**. Whatever it's shade or tint, blue is the colour associated with peace.

Yellow

Vibrant and radiant yellow has movement and **energy**. The first colour of spring imbues happiness, generating warmth and a feeling of well being. To understand the colour yellow and it's **impact**, think of the sun and the brilliance that it brings, creating **excitement** rather than providing a place of comfort. For this reason, we often find yellow in a family room or child's room.

Colour combining

The colour wheel is a simple, practical device which helps you to understand the relationship between colour and all its variations. Whether you depend on the wheel for guidance, or simply use it for inspiration, it is an essential decorating tool. The colour wheel features the primary colours positioned at an equal distance from each other around a circle. To make secondary colours, mix two primary colours together to create three new colours; mix red and blue to create violet; mix red and yellow to create orange and mix blue and yellow to create green. There is a third group of colours, called tertiary colours. These come from mixing a primary colour with a secondary colour and there are six colours in this group: saffron (red and orange); purple (red with violet); lime (yellow and green – although this colour can also be created by replacing the green with a little blue as on p.24); amber (yellow and orange); lavender (blue with violet); turquoise (blue with green). Tones and variations of a colour are sandwiched between the primary colours and are known as related colours, whilst complementary colours lie directly opposite each other. When used as a scheme, related colours will create a harmonious effect and complementary colours used together will often create strong dramatic effects. It is also possible to create tints by adding white to any colour (or indeed any colour to white to achieve the very popular "hint of" feel) and to add black to a colour to create a darker version or shade.

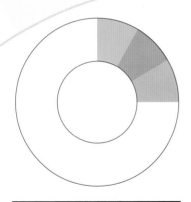

RELATED COLOURS

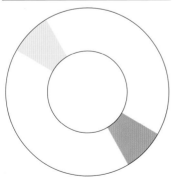

COMPLEMENTARY COLOURS

Colour combining

Mixing Paint

When mixing your own paints, the key is to not to be heavy handed but to mix slowly and gently a small amount at a time, as extra colour can always be added but not taken away. Take time to experiment with different combinations. You will find you can achieve a completely different second colour by varying the quantity of the two base colours. For instance, yellow plus a little red makes a light orange, whereas red plus a little yellow makes a terra-cotta red.

Orange (yellow plus red) plus white makes pale orange.

Yellow plus a little red makes light orange.

Yellow plus a little blue makes lime green.

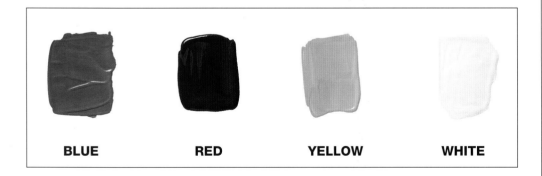

BLUE   **RED**   **YELLOW**   **WHITE**

Strong dark red plus white makes Old Rose pink.

Light red (red plus yellow) plus white makes terra-cotta.

Blue plus white makes pale, ice blue.

Green (blue plus yellow) plus white makes almond green.

Red plus a little yellow makes a terra-cotta red.

Red plus blue makes dull purple.

Purple (red plus blue) plus white makes soft lilac.

Green (blue plus yellow) plus red and white makes fawn.

Blue plus a little yellow makes blue-green.

Blue plus a little red makes indigo blue.

Purple (red plus blue) plus yellow and white makes taupe.

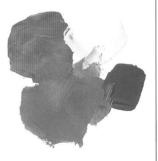

Orange (yellow plus red) plus white and blue makes olive.

Colour combining

Toning schemes

With no sudden colour change, these schemes create an impression of light and space. They will give a feeling of calm and quiet to a room and are best used to make small rooms look lighter or to make dark areas appear more open.

Harmonious schemes

Colours found next to each other on the colour wheel will create a calming and soothing atmosphere. Use them to create a fresh and spacious look.

Contrasting schemes

Colours found at the opposite end of the colour wheel will create a dramatic look, which is exciting and energizing. If you choose a contrasting colour scheme your room will be vibrant and upbeat.

Colour combining

Warm and cool colours

Warm colours are grouped together on the colour wheel – they contain elements of yellow and red. Warm colours can make a surface appear to advance and a room seem small and intimate. Cool colours contain elements of blue and green, making a surface appear to recede from the viewer, and a room seem larger.

Light and dark colours

A light coloured surface reflects more light than a dark coloured surface. Consequently rooms that are painted in a light colour will appear more open and larger than they really are. Even a warm colour can have this effect if it contains enough white. Dark colours absorb light, define spaces and make a room appear smaller.

Colour combining

Neutral colours

Neutral colours – black, white and grey – do not appear on the colour wheel. Other colours with a great deal of white or black, such as beige and cream, are also called neutrals. Neutral colours can provide the backdrop for other colours, or they can be used alone to create a harmonious scheme.

Preparation and Equipment

Preparation

Before you begin, it is important to consider the preparation and whilst this is not the most exciting of jobs and can be very time consuming – it is, I am afraid an area where you cannot cut corners if you want to achieve the best results. The level of the end product will reward the time and effort that you invest on preparation.

When painting a room, one of the first things to do is to ensure that anything that can be removed is. Taking furnishings and furniture out of the room at the start will save moving these from one side of the room to another every time you move onto a different wall. If there are items that cannot be removed, ensure that these are moved into a central position. You will need more space than you would envisage to paint a wall as it is important to have the freedom to move around at ground level, and also at ceiling level via a stepladder, so ensure that you leave sufficient space to move the ladder, and to climb up and down from the ladder.

Any items of furniture that remain in the room will need to be covered completely and whilst most of us are tempted to use old sheets to cover items, paint can sometimes saturate the material causing damage to furniture underneath, so unless you invest in

Preparation

professional dust sheets it is advisable to use strong plastic or polythene sheets. If it is practical, protect your carpet by rolling this back and then covering with a dustsheet. If however this is not an option, cover the floor with fabric dustsheets or old newspaper, overlapping each piece and taping it together. Do not be tempted to use plastic as this will create a slippery surface.

It is also important to protect the areas close to or adjoining the surface you will be painting, such as door frames, skirting boards and light fittings. The best way to do this is to apply masking tape, which has a specially formulated adhesive, which allows the tape to be applied and removed without damaging the paintwork. With short strips, mask off those areas you are not painting. Leave the tape in place until the paint around it is dry to touch, but do not leave for too long as you may find it damaging those surfaces it was intended to protect.

Remember to ensure that the room you are working in is well lit and ventilated. When possible, use natural daylight aided by portable work lamps and ensure that all available doors and windows are open.

If you are painting a piece of furniture, ensure that you have sufficient space to work and that the item (if possible) is positioned on a work bench or work surface for ease of application. Do not be tempted to move the article into the garden, however sunny the

Preparation

day, as this increases the chance of dust, pollen or even insects inadvertently attaching themselves to your masterpiece! Grease also resists paint so it is advisable to wipe over the area you are painting with a cloth and cleaning agent. You can buy specialist products from stores, or alternatively use a general household detergent, which will do the job just as well. Depending on the item you are painting, it may be necessary to remove old layers of paint with chemical strippers and in this instance, always refer to and follow the manufacturers instructions.

Blemishes, scratches and holes on walls or furniture also need to be repaired before you can begin to paint. Apply a generous amount of filler, as this will shrink slightly, to any crack and flatten with a trowel, working the filler in. Once the filler has dried completely, wrap a piece of sandpaper around a block of wood and move in circular motions until the surface is completely flat. There are many different types of sandpaper so it is important to use the right one whether you are sanding down fillers or preparing a surface to accept a primer, and generally this information is on the packaging.

Primers can be the difference between the amateur and the professional finish as they provide a barrier against moisture and dirt. Different surfaces require different primers and there are two main types – oil-based and water-based. Most are white, but you can tint them to resemble the colour of your final effect and the type of finish you decide upon will dictate the primer that you use. For instance oil and water-based paints will stick to a water-based primer, but a water-based paint will not stick to an oil primer.

Preparation

Once the surface has been cleaned and primed, apply the base coat. This will provide a smooth layer upon which to paint. If you are applying two base coats, ensure that the first coat is completely dry before adding the second layer. Particles of dust and dirt in the air may well end up on the surface you are painting. If this happens, remove the grit with the corner of a knife whilst the paint is still wet and then brush out the mark. If the paint is dry and you have noticed particles trapped in the paint, use fine-grade sandpaper to clean the area and then apply a thin layer of fresh paint, ensuring that it is blended into the surrounding area. It is easier to repair runs and drips in paint if the surface is still wet, so step back from your project every 15 minutes or so to check, and if there are any, simply smooth them out with a brush. However, if the run has become tacky, leave to dry and then sand out any imperfections, touching-up as and where necessary.

Equipment

It isn't necessary to spend a fortune on equipment, but you should, wherever possible, buy the best quality products you can afford to ensure good results. Before you begin a project, make sure that you have all of the tools and equipment necessary. There is nothing worse than finding half way through a job that you don't have what you need.

Brushes

Don't go out and buy every brush under the sun. Good quality paintbrushes will have very compact bristles and if you brush these against the palm of your hand there will be a notable tension before they spring back into shape. A poorer quality brush will lose bristles easily and result

in loose hairs being left in the paint. There are two types of brushes; natural bristles and synthetic. Natural brushes are made from animal hair whilst synthetic are made from either nylon or polyester, and occasionally a combination of the two. Generally you use a natural brush for oil-based paints, not for water-based, as the bristles will hold the water and the brush will be ruined. The width of bristles on a brush determines it's suitability, but it is fairly obvious that the finer or narrower the brush, the smaller area it is designed for, whilst wider brushes are more suited to larger areas.

There are certain paint effects that require specialist brushes, such as stencilling, where you will probably need to invest in a good quality brush, but you can achieve a lot of effects with general brushes. The key to ensuring that you do not have to reinvest in brushes every time you take on a different project is proper care and maintenance. There is no reason why a good quality brush

Equipment

cannot last years, as long as the paint is thoroughly removed after use and stored correctly. However, if you are planning on restarting or finishing a project the next day, there is no need to clean the brush. Simply place the brush and other equipment in a plastic bag whilst still wet, then secure the bag and make it airtight. Once you have finished your project, remove most of the excess paint from the brush by dragging it back and forth across a newspaper, then clean the brush with either white spirit (for oil-based paints) or hot running water for water-based. Making sure that the paint is removed from the brush is a messy job, you will need to fan out all of the bristles and wipe the handle with a rag dipped in cleaning solution, but it is worth your while. Remove any traces of solvent by washing in hot soapy water then hang up to dry. In order to further protect the bristles, once the brush is completely dry wrap it in kitchen paper so that the bristles are kept straight, then place an elastic band around the bristles to keep them tight.

Paint

To achieve the required effect and finish, it is essential that you use the right type of paint. Basically, paint can be broken down into two categories – water-based paints and oil-based paints – and the label on the tin of paint you buy will give you all the information you need. For instance, the label will specify whether the paint is oil or water-based and

Equipment

which surfaces the paint is suitable for and will provide advice on health, safety and preparation.

Water-based paints are used on walls, ceilings and woodwork and are suitable for use on any surface previously painted. Most people prefer to use these as they have a short drying time, which means that you can apply two coats in a day. Also, equipment and brushes are easier to clean than with an oil paint.

There are also a number of specialist paints available that will assist in creating decorative effects.

Stencil paint

These paints are water-based and easy to apply, but should be used sparingly. It is possible to use household paint for stencilling, but ready-mixed stencil paints have a better consistency for this popular paint effect.

Acrylic paint

Another type of water-based paint, acrylics are usually found in tube form and have a variety of interesting colours and finishes, such as metallic.

Fabric paint

Again, available in a wide range of colours and finishes, these are easy to apply and can also be sealed to withstand washing and ironing. Follow the label instructions clearly for information on usage.

Oil-based paint sticks

These can be used for stencilling but are not as easy to use as they appear (they look like wax crayons) and do take about 3 days to dry. To use them, break the protective seal and rub the colour onto the corner of your stencilling sheet. You will then need to use a brush to pick up the paint and apply in the normal way to the stencil.

Equipment

Cloths

Not only are these useful for cleaning brushes, but they are used in certain paint effects. If possible, buy mutton cloth by the roll, as this is lint free and will not leave fluff everywhere.

Sponges

General decorating sponges are not only useful when preparing surfaces for decoration, but can also be adapted and used to create "stamping" paint effects as well as a more soft-edged approach to stencilling. Natural sea sponges are also needed to create the classic "sponge" effect.

Masking tape

As mentioned previously, this is essential for protecting areas you do not want to paint and is also a very useful tool when

stencilling as it enables you to mask off areas of the stencil that you may wish to treat with a different colour. It is also great for repairing torn stencil templates.

Repositioning spray

This is for use when stencilling as it holds the template in place on the surface you are working on with a light adhesive, which prohibits paint from seeping under the bridges of the stencil.

Tracing paper

This is needed to trace around templates (p.84) for use when stencilling or stamping. If you can get tracing paper with grid lines, you can then enlarge the images you have traced.

Equipment

Enough paint to finish the job. Batches of the same brand and colour may still vary slightly in shade, so it is advisable to have too much rather than not enough. Most DIY stores will refund an unopened paint tin if you keep your receipt.

Taken all the necessary preparation steps. Remove all furniture, fixtures and fittings where necessary and cover the remaining items with dust sheets Make sure that you have sufficient light (you can always add to this with portable work lights) and that the room you are working in is well ventilated.

WHEN YOU HAVE COMPLETED THE PROJECTS, ENSURE THAT YOU DO THE FOLLOWING

Clean all tools and equipment. Extra diligence and thorough cleaning and drying of equipment will ensure that you are not making unnecessary costly purchases each time you take on a painting project. Remember also to store your equipment out of the reach of children, particularly if you are keeping any paints or solvents.

Dispose of excess paint safely. Whilst it is likely that you may wish to keep any leftover paint, if and when you decide to throw this away, do not pour old oil based paints down the drain. This is a hazardous substance and you will need to contact your local DIY store or council who will give you advice and information on how to dispose of this safely.

GLOSSARY OF EFFECTS

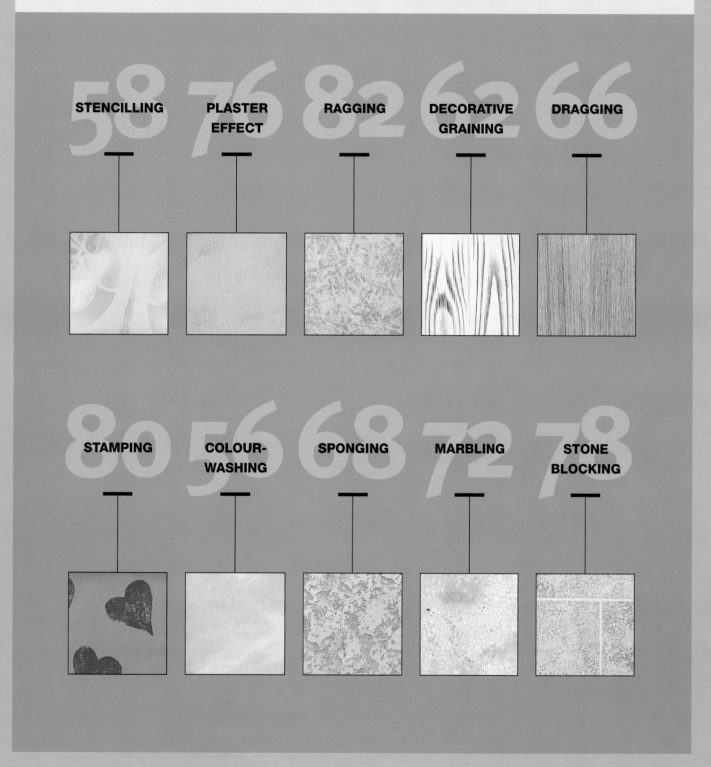

58 STENCILLING

76 PLASTER EFFECT

82 RAGGING

62 DECORATIVE GRAINING

66 DRAGGING

80 STAMPING

56 COLOUR-WASHING

68 SPONGING

72 MARBLING

78 STONE BLOCKING

Projects

Colour-washing

Colour-washing is one of the easiest and quickest ways of transforming any surface. The effect can be achieved by using either a water-based paint diluted with water, or an oil-based paint diluted with white spirit (see project below) and different variations of the effect can be achieved by either using a brush or a cloth to apply the second coat of paint. The beauty of this effect is the illusion of texture created means that walls or surfaces do not have to be perfectly smooth. The uneven look, ranging from light to dark shades, ensures that any imperfections are hidden.

On new panelling it is important to let the natural wood grain show through so there is no need to prepare with a base coat. However, it is essential to seal any knots that the wood may have with the relevant preparation to prevent any wood resins seeping through the paint.

Dilute the two colours to be used with an equal quantity of white spirit in the paint kettle. Apply the darkest colour directly onto the panelling first. Brush the paint outwards so the colour is stronger in some areas and lighter in others.

When the first coat is completely dry apply the second colour in the same way. Leave stronger patches of colour in some areas but work the paint well into other areas for a softer look. Take care to avoid making an obvious pattern.

MATERIALS
2 oil-based paint colours • White spirit • Paint kettle • 5cm/2in paint brush

---

HINT
When attempting this effect on a plastered wall, use a large 15cm/6in brush and apply the paint in sweeping criss-cross motions. Dry the brush and sweep over the walls whilst the paint is still wet.

Stencilling

Possibly the most popular paint effect of recent years, due no doubt to the fact that beginners and experts alike are able to alter drastically their decoration and living environment with this very simple method. The cost of stencilling however can escalate with the need for specialist paints and brushes, not to mention the expense of pre-cut stencils. It is actually very easy to make your own stencils with a few basic materials bought from craft shops. The most durable and user friendly type of stencil is made from acetate as this enables you to clearly see the positioning of the template, and it is easy to cut your own designs from these sheets with a craft knife. A selection of stencilling templates is provided at the back of the book.

Stencilled clock

For this project, an old wooden cupboard from a junk shop has been transformed into a clock, but stencilling, but can be adapted for any surface, including walls and fabric. Paint two contrasting colours of emulsion paint onto the wooden surface. Draw the circular clock face by tracing around a saucer and paint it cream. Simulate age by lightly rubbing the surface with sandpaper.

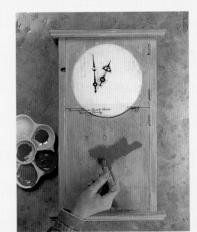

Position the first stencil layer onto the front of the cupboard using positioning spray and stencil a solid layer of green for the tree and blue for the birds. When the paint is dry reposition the stencil to align with the previously stencilled areas. Next apply the third colour as a solid block as this will add to its naïve charm.

Using a pencil and ruler, work out the position of the numbers on the clock face using a dark colour. Depending on the size of your clock you can stencil some, or all of the numbers. Distress the stencilled areas with sandpaper to remove the newness of the paint and fix the clock hands and mechanism in place.

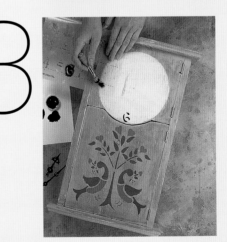

MATERIALS

Emulsion paints • 5cm/2in paint brush • Plate/saucer • Pencil • Sandpaper
Stencil • Repositioning spray • Stencil paints • Stencil brushes • Palette
Clock hands and mechanism • Ruler

HINT

Take care not to slide the stencil when positioning or moving it across your project as this may smudge the paint.

Stencilling

Marquetry effect floorboards

As a border on bare wooden floors this stencil design imitates the marquetry effect and belies the true simplicity of the project.

Create a border for the stencil design by carefully placing two strips of masking tape on the floor about 5cm/2in apart. Fill in the gap between the tape with the darkest shade of varnish. Be sparing with the varnish on the brush and work from the inside of the gap outwards to the edges in a brisk dabbing motion. When dry, carefully peel away the masking tape.

Choose a stencil that uses at least two different colours and ensure that your stencil template is solvent resistant. Position the stencil sheet against the bottom edge of the varnish stripe and paint through the stencil with coloured varnish onto the floorboards. Remove the template and wash away any varnish residue. When the first application of varnish is dry, reposition the template and hold in place with masking tape, ensuring that you have matched the lines of the design accurately. Now, apply the second coloured varnish.

Lastly, allow 24 hours for the varnishes to completely dry and then paint the whole of the design with a coat or two of clear gloss varnish to protect from scuffs.

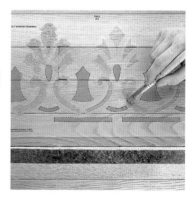

MATERIALS

3 colours wood varnish • Stencil brushes • Stencils • Masking tape
Clear gloss varnish • White spirit

HINT

If necessary, add artist's oil colours to the varnish to achieve the required shade of varnish.

Stencilling

Leaf and berry wall decoration

From a distance this stencil may look like wallpaper, but it has far more character, particularly if you vary the pressure on the brush for lighter and darker leaves.

Place the thin paper over the leaf and berry design shown at the end of the book and trace around the outline with a pencil. Repeat the outline using ink so that the design will register underneath a photocopier and then enlarge to the required size. Lightly spray the stencil sheet with repositioning spray and place over the photocopy. Place this onto a cutting board and with the craft knife carefully cut out the design.

Position and secure the plumb line and line the stencil up against this. Secure the stencil to the wall and apply the paint. When the first application has been completed, peel the template from the wall and reposition the template directly below the completed image. As you stencil remember to vary the pressure on the brush for an interesting effect.

Work your way around the room in a clockwise direction, moving the plumb line and checking the distance between the stripes with a tape measure before stencilling. Arrange the stencils so the decoration faces upward for the first stripe, and then downward for the next and so on until you have finished.

MATERIALS

Pencil • Tape measure • Plumb line • Thin paper • Ink pen • Stencil sheet
Repositioning spray • Craft knife • Cutting board • Stencil paint
Plate/palette • Stencil brush • Tape measure

HINT

Measure and mark the positions on your wall where you intend to stencil your design.

Hang a plumb line and use the string as a guide to position the edge of the stencil.

1

2

3

Decorative graining

Woodgraining, most commonly used on doors, is a technique that imitates the properties of real wood with combed and brushed glazes combined to create realistic effects. Acrylic paint is applied to door panels and allowed to dry, then an acrylic glaze is added and brushed using gentle sweeping motions. In this way, mock mahogany, oak and pine effects can be achieved by varying the colour of glaze and brush or comb. Unlike woodgraining, where the aim is to create a natural effect, the project below illustrates decorative graining which intentionally creates a dramatic artificial effect. Experiment with different colours and patterns to create striking yet simple designs.

1

Prepare the cupboard by removing any remaining old paint and sanding down if necessary. Apply two layers of the base coat paint, allowing each to dry thoroughly, and lightly sand down between each application.

2

Mix equal quantities of the white emulsion with the glaze in a paint kettle and blend well. Apply the mixed glaze over the central panels of the cupboard only, as the remainder of the cupboard is left plain.

3

Using the rubber wood graining tool, pull through the wet glaze, starting at the top of the panel and working slowly downwards. Rock the tool gently back and forth as you progress down the panel to achieve the dramatic grained effect.

MATERIALS
Coloured emulsion paint – base coat • White emulsion paint – top coat
5cm/2in paint brush • Rubber wood graining tool • Fine grade sandpaper
Paint kettle

HINT
If you are not happy with the effect, brush over the glaze while it is still wet and attempt the technique again.

Dragging

Unlike colour washing which can hide imperfections, it is imperative that the surface you choose to drag is completely smooth and even. One of the more traditional effects, this technique is particularly suited for use on panelled doors as the fine dragged lines follow the panels. However, as doors are in constant use it is advisable to use an oil-based paint which is more hardwearing, although impressive results can also be achieved with a water-based paint and acrylic glaze. It takes a little time and practice to avoid obvious brush marks at the point where dragging starts. Use your free hand to hold the bristles firmly against the glazed surface until the brush starts to make its own mark.

Prepare the door by sanding down thoroughly and if necessary filling any cracks with wood filler. Paint with two layers of the base coat, allowing to dry between each. Dilute the top coat in a paint kettle with one part paint to one part oil glaze.

Using the dragging brush, apply a thin layer of coloured glaze to the door. Work with long vertical strokes to correspond with the direction of the dragging. You can paint the entire door as the glaze remains moveable for some time.

Start working with the door panels first. Draw the brush from top to bottom, maintaining an even pressure and keeping the brush strokes as parallel as possible. Finish by dragging the upright and horizontal bars then finally the door frame.

1

2

3

MATERIALS

Oil-based primer • White oil-based paint – base coat

Coloured oil-based paint – top coat • Transparent oil glaze • White spirit

Paint brush • Dragging brush or long haired paint brush • Paint kettle • Sandpaper

---

HINT

If your lines look uneven or wobbly, start again immediately before the glaze has a chance to dry.

Sponging

Sponged walls

Prepare the surface that you will be painting and apply two base coats of your chosen colour. Allow the base coat to dry thoroughly and then mix each of the colours you will be sponging in a mixing container with one part paint to one part water.

Pour some of the darkest sponging paint and water mix into the paint tray and dip in the sponge, being careful not to allow too much paint to get onto the sponge. It is easier to add more paint to a wall than to remove too much! If the sponge has collected too much paint, dab the sponge on an old newspaper to remove the excess. Dab the sponge lightly on the wall, turning the angle of your hand slightly after each application to give a varied effect. Ensure that you leave small spaces between each mark.

Allow the first sponging layer to dry and then repeat the process with the second darkest paint. This time, make sure that any obvious gaps left from the first colour are filled in, and that the colour is evenly overlapping. Repeat the process all over again with the lightest colour. Remember this time around that what you see is what you get by way of a finished effect, so stand back from the project regularly and adjust the positioning of the sponge marks accordingly.

MATERIALS

Natural sea sponge • Emulsion paint – base colour

2/3 shades of emulsion paint – sponging • Mixing container • Shallow paint tray

---

HINT

Always wash the sponge between each application of paint to ensure the individual colour retains its definition.

Marbling

There are many different types of marble and as a result there are probably as many techniques for marbling. Like woodgraining, this is a technique where a surface is painted to resemble another. The best way to achieve a realistic result is to study examples of real marble, and it is useful to have a piece of marble (such as a pastry board) to refer to when creating this effect. The project below breaks down the basic principles to make a simplified version that always follows three basic steps; applying the glaze, distressing the glaze and veining.

Prepare the area for painting by "keying" the surface with fine sandpaper. Apply two layers of the base coat, allowing each to dry thoroughly. Mix a little raw sienna colour with about one tablespoon each of white spirit and oil glaze in a paint kettle and paint sparingly over the area with a soft artist's brush.

Wrap the cotton cloth into a small pad and wipe away varying sized "pebble" shapes from the wet glaze, allowing patches of light and dark to form. To achieve a real marble effect, rub off long thin shapes surrounded by clusters of smaller round shapes.

To create the "veins" of the marble, thin the raw umber colour with a little white spirit and then apply this with the fine long-haired artist's brush. Use the tip of the brush for fine veins, and apply slightly more pressure to create thicker ones. Soften the veins by going over these with a soft brush, blending gently into the background colour. When dry, use a high gloss vanish to seal and protect the marbling.

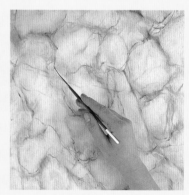

MATERIALS

Oil-based paint – base coat • Transparent oil glaze • Tubes of artist's oil colour (raw sienna and raw umber) • White spirit • 5cm/2in paint brush • Cotton cloth Fine-grade sandpaper • Soft artist's brush • Fine artist's brush • Paint kettle

---

HINT

Ensure that you hold the brush loosely when veining otherwise the lines created with be too harsh.

Marbling

Marbled panelling

This marbling technique uses quick-drying emulsion paints and the panelling is made from pieces of wallpaper. This means you can work on a flat surface then simply cut and paste the panels to the wall.

Apply white emulsion base coat to the wallpaper. Mix equal amounts of the coloured emulsion with the glaze and paint onto the wallpaper with a wide brush. While the glaze is still wet, twist a cotton cloth into a sausage shape and place onto the glazed surface. Roll off the glaze as if you were rolling pastry! Shake out and retwist the cloth occasionally, following the same direction all the time until you have ragged the whole surface.

Add a little artist's acrylic paint to darken the top colour and mix with a little glaze and water. Paint sparingly in a diagonal direction from left to right, then right to left across the paper. Soften the edges by brushing lightly with a dry long-haired paint brush.

Use an artist's fine paint brush dipped in the white base colour to paint diagonal veins across the surface of the softened bands of colour. While these veins are still wet, lightly stroke with a feather to soften their outline. When dry, finish with a high gloss varnish and then affix to the wall.

M a t e r i a l s

White emulsion paint – base coat • Vinyl wallpaper

2 colours emulsion paint – top coats • Emulsion glaze

Tube of artist's acrylic paint • Cotton cloth • 5cm/2in paint brush

Long-haired paint brush for softening

Artist's fine paint brush • Feather • Paint kettle • High gloss varnish

Plaster effect

This technique is called plaster effect because when the three colours are combined they give a lovely soft appearance, similar to that of new plasterwork.

Paint the walls using two base coats of white emulsion, then mix together each of the three coloured top coats with equal quantities of glaze and water. Blend each mixture well in separate paint kettles. Pour a little of the darkest paint and glaze mix into a paint tray. Dip the sponge lightly into this and apply it to the surface using a circular "scrubbing" action to create a cloudy layer of colour. This effect takes practice but the result is better than using a paint brush.

When the surface is dry, apply the second, medium coloured paint and glaze mix. This should be applied sparingly to maintain a cloudy layer while allowing the underlying colour to show through in patches. If the second colour is too dense, rub off with a clean cloth.

When dry, apply the lightest paint and glaze mix. Again this is applied very sparingly and is intended simply to soften the whole effect while giving just a hint of colour. If at this stage you feel the overall effect is too light, reapply the first colour.

1

2

3

MATERIALS

White emulsion paint – base coat

Light, medium and dark emulsion paint – top coats • Emulsion glaze

Cellulose decorator's sponge • Paint tray • Paint kettles

Stone-blocking

This technique can take quite a time to measure out, however, the effect can be most unusual. The imitation stone has a dignity, which is well suited to formal rooms, but for a less dramatic effect, try this around a fireplace.

Apply two coats of the ivory emulsion to the wall. This will eventually show through as the "grouting" between the fake stonework. Work out the size of your blocks on paper first, then using a spirit level, set square and ruler, mark out the pattern on the wall. Mask off each block, placing the masking tape to the right of each vertical pencil mark and below each horizontal pencil mark.

Your choice of coloured emulsions should ideally resemble the colour of stone. Mix the medium coloured emulsion with an equal part of glaze in a paint tray and sponge evenly over the area you have marked, including the masking tape. Allow to dry completely. Next, mix the darker emulsion with an equal quantity of glaze and using a clean sponge apply over the first colour, overlapping in irregular shaped patches to vary the density of colour. Allow to dry.

Mix the lightest emulsion, again with equal quantities of the glaze, and apply randomly over the entire surface to soften the previous colours. When this last application has dried remove the masking tape. Peel very carefully to ensure that you do not lift off the ivory base coat or "grouting".

1

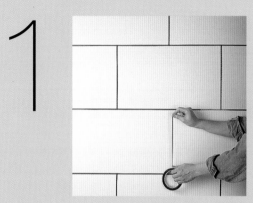

2

3

MATERIALS

Ivory coloured emulsion paint – base coat

Light, medium and dark emulsion paint – top coat • Emulsion glaze

Masking tape • Ruler • Pencil • Sea sponge • Paint tray

Spirit level • Set square

Stamping

Stamping is growing in popularity, the main reason being the simplicity and effectiveness of this technique. It is also incredibly versatile and can be adapted to virtually any surface, which makes it possible to co-ordinate stamps on walls and soft furnishings. Stamps can be made of a number of materials including lino, rubber, foam, sponge and even potatoes and other vegetables. As with most paint effects, it is important not to put too much paint onto the stamp, so once you have prepared your surface and chosen your stamp design and colour of your paint, test the sponge on an old newspaper to gauge the effect. Certain types of stamps create different imprints, so choose the one most suitable to your needs. A cellulose decorator's sponge, which is dense in texture, will give a more defined stamp than a natural sea sponge.

To create your stamp, trace a template from the section at the back of the book. Draw over the traced line on the back of the tracing paper and then trace the image onto a sheet of white paper. Carefully cut out the paper template following the traced outline. If you are making a stamp from a potato, cut the potato in half and then draw your design straight onto the potato. Very carefully, cut around the design, removing the background.

Using the fine marker pen, draw around the template onto the sponge. Take extra care to ensure that you have as clean a line as possible. To achieve the best results when stamping, it is important that the "stamp" retains its original shape.

Using a pair of sharp scissors, cut out the sponge stamp and neaten any rough edges. Pour the paint into the tray, then with a small sponge roller apply the paint to the stamp, ensuring an even covering without saturation. You may need to test the stamp on scrap paper or newspaper, and once you are happy with the result apply the stamp firmly to the wall. Do not press too hard as this will blur the outline of your design.

MATERIALS

Tracing paper • Paper • Pencil • Fine marker pen • Scissors • Cellulose sponge • Emulsion and fabric paints • Small sponge roller • Paint tray

---

Ragging

With this simple, yet effective, technique, you can completely alter the appearance of furniture, creating some very interesting effects. This particular technique involves applying a layer of glaze to an item and then using a rag to lift off the glaze (illustrated below). You can also roll the rag back and forth across the surface you are decorating, however you must ensure there is an overlap on the rows that you roll. The material you choose as your rag will result in a different effect, so experiment with different types, but remember to remove any old buttons if you are using old clothing. Also, it is essential that you have plenty of "rags" to hand, as whatever material you use will quickly become saturated with paint.

Ragged chair

Ensure that the area of object that you are going to paint is thoroughly cleaned then apply two coats of your chosen base colour, allowing the first to dry completely before the next application.

In a mixing container, mix equal amounts of the glaze and white topcoat. With a brush, apply a thin coating of this onto your project. If you are painting furniture, ensure that the glaze does not build up around the corners.

Loosely crumple the cloth and press onto the wet glaze. As you lift off the cloth from the surface, you remove portions on the glaze. Repeat the process with swift movements until the project is completed. When the cloth is covered with glaze, shake it out and recrumple before continuing.

MATERIALS

Coloured oil-based paint – base coat • White oil-based paint – top coat

Transparent oil glaze • Paint brush • Cotton rag • White spirit

Sandpaper • Paint kettle

Templates

Templates

Templates

ABCDEFGHIJ
KLMNOPQR
STUVWXYZ
1234567890